# Ms informed™

## Wake Up Wisdom For Women

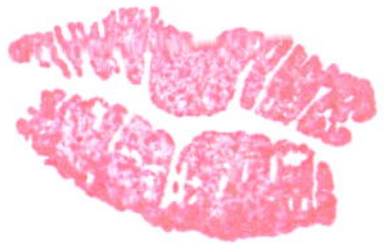

Ms. Oh Gosh! Productions

ISBN 978-0-9833927-0-5



Book's Website: http://www.MsInformed.co



Ms. Informed books are available at special quantity discounts for corporate education and training use.

For more information, email: info@msinformed.co

## Dedication

In knowing, working with and presenting to so many capable women over the years, it became apparent to me that we all could use a good shot of confidence. Life is hard enough without us being hard on ourselves.

Therefore, this book is dedicated to all those wonderful women and other women who are exceptionally creative, smart and inspirational in so many ways but lack the ability to be truly proud of their contributions to the world. I hope the information in this book helps them to shine even brighter.

Don't let me or anyone else tell you how to live your life or that you aren't doing your best already. My hope is that you will find confirmation of things you never, or only slightly, considered that are brutally true but immediately helpful. With that knowledge and comfort, you'll realize that you are quite fine. With that wisdom, I pray that you can laugh more, sleep better and live happily ever after.

*A portion of the profits from Ms. Informed will be donated to The Glamour Project http://www.glamourproject.org.*

*With make-up and props in hand, Glamour Project volunteers go to women's homeless shelters to give each woman a makeup application, fashion styling and professional glamour shot as a means for these women to reclaim their confidence, beauty and sense of hope.*

## Table of Contents

# Ms. conduct

## Surveys, lies and videotapes

In January 2011, we surveyed 195 women ages 20-80 using an online tool and careful means to ensure complete confidentiality for all survey participants.

Throughout this book we will share the results of the survey as well as other data points that will be sourced. Because of the subjectivity of the information, the data is not intended to provide empirical proof of any trend, or even to imply there is a right or wrong answer to the questions asked. The data is presented here simply as validation about what other women are claiming to do and think.

It is possible that you are not going to agree, appreciate or you may even be offended by some of the harsh truths uncovered by the data or in my commentary. You are certainly entitled to your opinion as I am mine. So whether the discussions confirm your existing beliefs and behaviors or if they stir you to make a change for the better, may the words hereafter serve you well.

# Ms.behaved

## We all need a grown-up time-out

I am confident that you are not.

None of us are.

Unfortunately, mankind as a whole is an insecure species and its woman-folk don't parlay other people's insecurities into an advantage as well as their macho earth mates.

As women, we are taught to be caregivers and therefore, by default, to be selfless and literally less of self. This causes us to feel perpetually guilty and, ironically, in need of perpetual help. We seek life and business coaches, therapy, meditation, support groups, and even drugs to gain perspective and regain confidence. Worse, our insecurities make us do some really foolish and unproductive things to ourselves and to others. We gossip, we obsess, we worry and we constantly put our high heels in our own lip-glossed mouths. The good thing is: You are not alone. We all do it. So shut up, Kermit — being green is so much easier.

In general, most men are encouraged to be independent and indifferent to other people's feelings. "Cocky" is usually a backhand compliment to a guy implying he has confidence both physically and socially (perhaps cause and effect?). As a result, men are irreverent. They just move on. We womenfolk, however, we belabor, we analyze, and we talk about things until we are convinced that we are powerless to do anything more than rationalize.

For example, like anyone, I bet you've been dissed more times than you want to remember. By "dissed" I mean someone (a friend, colleague or relative — we'll call her Mary) said something negative behind your back to another person (let's call her Alice). Hearing the negative comment from Mary, Alice then comes and informs you about what Mary said. I bet your first reaction was to ask yourself, "Why did Mary say that?"; "What did I do that caused her to say that?"; "Could Mary have misunderstood something I did or didn't do?"; "Did I misspeak or misunderstand something?" You probably got completely riled by the situation and tried to figure it out by talking to other friends to look for explanation, comfort, and alliance.

Eventually, someone asks you why Alice even told you about Mary's comment. Hmm…that is a good question! Alice assured you that she was only telling you "so that you were aware" — but come on! Did it really help in any way for you to know that Mary said anything in the first place? What was Alice's real reason for telling you? Was it to make you feel badly, or to make you mad at Mary — or both? Would it have been better for you to just not know? Probably!

So now you are miffed at both Mary and Alice — and even worse, you still feel horrible about yourself and what you did or didn't do to deserve this. Day and night your mind is replaying the scenario trying to figure out why it happened and how to deal with it. When you finally get the chance to talk to your husband, partner or another male and retell him the saga, his likely response is, "Just forget about it." OMG — doesn't he see how upset you are! Now you are totally pissed at him! How dare he minimize your agony!

I hope you are giggling because it's funny to read about it. But, yes, we have and continue to all be there. "We" women that is….

*"Great minds discuss ideas.*
*Average minds discuss events.*
*Small minds discuss people."*
— Eleanor Roosevelt

A man will usually just ignore small life speed bumps like this. When they do bump into something, they unemotionally steer around it or go another way because they feel that it's not that important. They believe that it's just easier to find another way. (Perhaps this is why they hate asking for driving directions, too.)

There is literally constitutional and legal confirmation that all men are created equal; and, therefore, they are as important as anyone else. This is not arrogance. It's the understanding that they have all the ingredients and rights to be as good as or better than anyone else. This means they often don't care much what other people say or think on a personal level. It means they don't usually assume another person's responsibility or even have interest in another's hang-ups or problems. And, yes, I am generalizing as there are exceptions (besides from wonderful gay men).

However, consider this: Ms. Liberty stands outside with her arms aching, coping with the natural elements all by herself. People she doesn't even know walk all over her day in and day out, but she continues her offer to take care of the tired, poor and huddled masses yearning to breathe free. Talk about a metaphor and a "Ms. Nomer!" That doesn't sound like 'liberty' to me! In contrast, perhaps you are old enough to remember Mr. Magoo. He was blissfully ignorant, eventually getting to where and what he wanted without the damaging stress most women impose on themselves today.

Women can learn a lot from this indifference. It can help remove the default assumption that failure of any kind is due to our own lack of competence. No one should live ignorantly or be too much of a Pollyanna, but perhaps we can become more resilient to things beyond our control. Self-doubt and concern for social acceptance is what prevents us from accomplishing things and its wastes time and energy.

My husband often tells me to let it roll off my back…how often I wonder what that would really feel like.

> Women ages 20-29 are least confident — 33% admit that they are not confident — while women over 60 are the most — 83.3% said they were confident. It turns out that women over 60 also reported being happier in general — 91.7% said they were happy with their lives now.

In observing so many women — business owners, working gals, mothers, wives, relatives, and friends — it never ceases to amaze me how deeply insecurities lay at the heart of all of our actions and thoughts. Jealousy, bitchiness, bullying, indecisiveness, addictions and all of Pandora's girlfriends' gifts are unfortunately part of the female deal that can, at best, be identified as feminine flaws. This robs us of going after the things we really want and can do that make us feel good and genuinely satisfied. We can blame our hormones, our mothers, our fate, or even our male relationships, but the real truth is that we lack the true self-esteem to overcome the constant yearning to be wanted by others.

As you will read on in the book, we are actually lucky because you will learn that Maslow's Theory applies to all humans and how our need belong affects everything we do. This means when people do selfish, seemingly stupid, and usually unproductive things to you and to others, you will then understand why so you can cope better. You will then be more able to support yourself and others that you care about. Once you recognize the culprit as insecurity, you will be able to account for and deal with your own and anyone else's undesirable behavior. Then, just maybe you'll spend less time and money on more self-help books, shrinks and happy pills.

*I truly believe that you are not broken.*

*You are simply misinformed.*

## Girl Talk Guidelines

1. How do you define confidence?

2. Name some people famous or not that you think are confident and how they demonstrate that.

3. Think about a time when you were dissed. What, and why, in retrospect, do you think it happened? How would you have handled it differently now looking back?

4. Has a lack of confidence held you back from doing something you really wanted to do? Why?

# Ms.aligned

## Chiropractors can't fix bonehead maneuvers

*"You will do foolish things, but do them with enthusiasm."*
— Colette
quoted in the Montreal Gazette

- Ever talk about someone behind her back?
- Ever brag to or one-up someone?
- Ever correct someone else in public?
- Ever give someone fake congratulations?
- Ever get angry at someone when they don't return a favor?
- Ever get pleasure at someone else's bad luck or unfortunate situation?

Of course you did — to some or all those things! We all did and do! Maybe you felt badly doing it, or perhaps secretly you felt vindicated. Most likely, you did experience some stress trying to justify why you did it.

Furthermore, one or more of those nasty things have been done to you, too. And that sucks…truly. It sucks because it's hurtful and it sucks because it sucks your energy, weighing on your conscious and confidence. It 'uber-sucks' when someone you trusted, like a friend, relative or work ally, does something mean spirited to you. Whether it's intentional or not, bonehead words or actions really set your defenses into overdrive and, therefore, cause stress.

So rather than lament about it (or in girl terms, "bitch" about it), let's understand why it happens and how we can dismiss it as just wasteful woman behavior. This won't make it stop happening to you or even stop you from doing it to someone else. But at least by understanding the cause, it may help you avoid the accompanying stress most of the time. More importantly, when it does happen, you'll know the reasons are not due to something you did or should have done. In other words, you will be able to acknowledge both the problem and the cause. When you feel the stress from a bonehead move, you'll be able to quickly dismiss it and move on (yes, we girls can do it, too!). Things may still not easily roll off your back, but at least you can start letting them slowly drip away.

### My quarter-million-dollar-man, Maslow

I have both good and bad takeaways from my educational experience at the notoriously competitive and results-driven Wharton Business School. Among my lessons were how to be resourceful and how utterly uncreative accounting is. However, Wharton taught me one academic idea that changed my life, and I know it will change yours, too. Just bear with me as we dive a little into theoretical waters so we can grab hold of this life buoy. It cost me about a quarter million dollars in student loans and work-study hours, but I happily give it to you here for the price of this book. I believe this is the key to helping you stay afloat when imbecile, bonehead maneuvers pull you down.

Abraham Maslow (April 1, 1908 – June 8, 1970) is considered to be the founder of humanistic psychology. His 1943 paper on human motivation was a study of sane, well-accomplished individuals and the means by which they succeeded. His paper has influenced modern psychology and management theory; and, more importantly, just makes sense to all of us struggling to be socially adept.

Maslow's premise is actually very simple. He theorized that there is an order and priority of human needs we must satisfy in order to be motivated and happy. He illustrated these needs in his now famous pyramid:

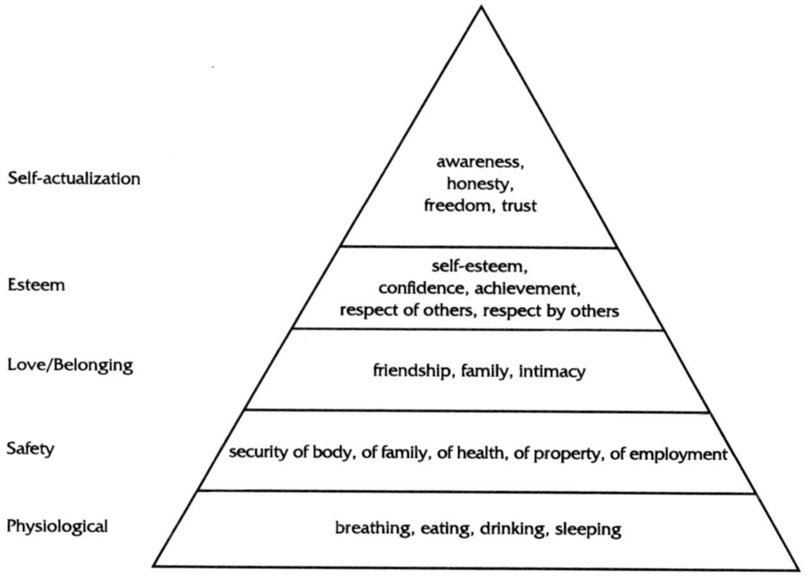


**Maslow's Hierarchy of [Human] Needs**

*Source: blog.MakingITClear.com*

It's easy to see that the first level, the physiological needs, are basic life functions such as food, water, and sleep (and, yes, indeed, he actually included sex! And, yes, we will talk much more about that in this book...so be ready!). Without those first level physiological needs met, we simply can't survive — and, anything above that isn't possible. Once those needs are met, you can progress up the pyramid to the next level and so on.

Level two is all about safety in terms of having shelter and knowing that you can provide for yourself and your loved ones. If you have food but live in a place that is unsafe from environmental elements or crime, or if you don't have means to get food, Maslow argues that you can't be happy. I have to agree (but can we include wine in that, too?) When we get laid off or have financial worries, this not only wreaks havoc on our egos, but directly impacts our ability to move up the pyramid and be happy.

At the top of the pyramid is intellectual mecca. This is the ability to use our brain cells on things other than survival (obtaining food and shelter) and be capable of creativity and spirituality. Maslow's Theory says that those areas of human ability are compromised if the bottom levels are not fulfilled.

This brings me back to the middle level labeled "love/belonging." The middle, and often overlooked level, is the one we struggle with the most day to day, and it the cause of most people's bonehead activity. We all have an inherent — as in, not optional — need to belong and to be loved.

This is essentially something we need in order to be happy and successful. We join synagogues, temples and churches, associations and clubs. We have friends and cliques, gangs, and teams. We buy many things we really don't need just because we want to be cool and "in". We do uncomfortable things because we don't want to be thought of as losers or "outcasts". Sometimes we agree to other people's ideas even if we have no opinion just so we are allied. I can argue that many people even have children and get married because they subconsciously need to belong to something other than themselves.

The good news is that this is the foundation of every society and it motivates us to procreate, recreate and relate our lives to a greater good. The bad news is that we often — perhaps even constantly — need to reassure ourselves that we actually do belong. When we doubt this, we tend to do foolish things.

For example, when we talk behind someone's back, it's because we want the person we are communicating with to like us better and make us feel more 'belonged' than the person we are talking about. When we get mad at others for not helping out, we assume it's because they don't care enough about us. It makes us feel unimportant and not part of the loving group we long to belong to. In fact, you can attribute most human behavior to someone's need to belong. People are motivated by this need and, therefore, do things that make them feel a stronger sense of belonging to something.

Maslow's Theory has been applied in many ways, including management theory, which is why I learned about it at Wharton. My professor demonstrated how you could motivate (some might say manipulate) other people to do things by understanding their fundamental Maslovian need and then making your request clearly in support of their desire.

For example, an airline ticket agent probably doesn't really "want" to help you, she 'needs' to as part of her job. So if you understand that and figure out how to motivate her to rebook your just-missed flight, you might approach your request differently knowing your problem isn't hers. For example, you might try something like this: "Ms. Riley, I know you must be very busy but I believe that you have the ability to help me fix this situation that would mean so much to me and the other people that are being unfortunately impacted until I get to Phoenix." In this way, you are asking her to use her professional superpowers to prove she can fix the problem. You are motivating her to do it because she'll be a hero to you and to other people. Men and women will find it hard to say no to such a subordinate request for help. They'll want to show off their power and gain a sense of purpose and belonging by being a part of the solution.

If taken to an extreme, when you belong to something, you have power over those who want to belong, too. This is why we have bullies and dictators. Therefore, you might even extend the need to belong to explain bigger issues like war and religious contention, but our mission here is to understand the more controllable problems in our lives: bonehead words and actions.

So my tuition-free, semester-in-a-book gift to you is to show you why and how our lives can be easier by remembering this profound concept from Maslow while we examine our many female roles:

- Employee or entrepreneur
- Student/mentee
- Friend
- Relative
- Girlfriend
- Mother
- Wife or partner

We'll look at the typical demoralizing things we do to ourselves and to others. We'll laugh and cry about how silly we can be. We'll also get pissed and inspired when we see the wasted energy and stress we cause. And, yes, we will talk about sex….!

## Girl Talk Guidelines

1. Have you ever felt like you wanted to literally crawl out of your own skin? When did this happen and what caused that feeling?

2. Consider a time when you were asking for someone's help and that person was utterly rude. Replay that experience and think about how you could have applied Maslovian concepts to manage that person differently.

3. Think about the people you know who often brag or otherwise must ensure that you are aware of their belongings or accomplishments. Can you figure out what causes them to need this recognition and belonging?

4. Consider all the ways that you fill your own need to belong. What organizations, relationships and other ways satisfy that need? Are they all providing enough personal fulfillment?

# Ms.cast

## Family, friends and other 'cat-ty' relationships

*"The chief barrier to happiness is envy."*

— Frank Tyger
quoted in Forbes.com

You expect your family and friends to be your fans. They may be, but they may also surprise you once in a while by dowsing your ideas or enthusiasm with their own jealous reactions. For example, did you ever share a new business concept or personal goal with a girlfriend or cousin only for her to react negatively? You expected her to be a cheerleader and she turned out to be a center tackle ready to plow over you and your idea. Why?

It turns out that this is a very common experience that many women share with me when I present and discuss it. They are haunted by the experiences that made them feel stupid, ashamed and disappointed.

> 90.6% of the women surveyed said they have at least once received a negative reaction from friends or relatives upon sharing news about a promotion, being engaged, getting pregnant or another accomplishment that the woman, herself, felt proud or happy about.

Yet, only 49% admit to doing it to someone else.

Maslow's Theory may explain that your female confidante felt insufficient in some way. As such, she pulled out her female claws and brought you down to her own level. In this way, she could feel OK about her own lack of good ideas. She can't compete, so she takes you out of the race. It may not even be totally intentional, but it's nonetheless harmful. The scars from these unexpected cat fights last a long time...sometimes for both femme felines.

### Sisters, mothers and aunts — oh my!

Like the animals feared in the Wizard of Oz, lions, tigers and bears are all fiercely protective of their immediate families. Even with members of the extended family, they will attack to the death if they need to defend their own babies and homes. Sisters, mothers and aunts aren't quite as ruthless but there may be real competition to have the best houses, the best kids, the best cars and so on. Additionally, every woman has a subconscious need to maintain her pack order in the overall extended family hierarchy. Between family members, some women play the role of peacemaker, some wind up being instigators. Some become the caregivers, while their relatives subsequently become "care takers".

It's no secret that families can be tough to deal with, but it's really hard when someone you love squashes your dreams. You can justify that person's ignorance or bad attitude, but it still stings and swells. More often than not, our surveyed women noted they were put down by their own mothers (and some fathers) and these women still haven't recovered, even decades later.

There seems to be no cure for the infection left by a mother's negative opinion. You may not even agree with her judgment, but you just can't rid yourself of that doubt.

Ever happen to you? It's happened to me several times, and it infuriated me every time. Often times, I can't seem to help myself in wanting to share my excitement with close female friends and relatives yet, the feedback sometimes comes back as: "Why would you want to do that? That's crazy." I almost didn't publish this book when a trusted friend questioned why anyone would even buy it. Luckily, I had my Maslovian armor on.

So, now we have to work hard to remind ourselves that our family and friends need to belong too. When we share a grand, new bandwagon idea that has the potential for fun and money, they may decide not to jump on it; but, rather, they tell us why it won't work and, in essence, rain on our parade. Perhaps this makes it easier for them to live with themselves. Perhaps they really don't like the idea. Perhaps someone else had burst their bubble in the past and its subconscious revenge. It may not be totally intentional on their part, and it may even be done in cloaked love.

**911 versus 711 friends**

So what about friends? Are they typically supportive of your new ideas and initiatives? Maybe not, for similar reasons as your relatives described above. However, with friends, there is always an option — either of you can opt out of the friendship. Relatives can't. Sure, relatives can ignore you or simply avoid participating in family functions; but legally, and perhaps socially, family is not usually optional. Besides, it is a major means by which we fulfill our Maslovian requirement to belong.

With friends, however, we choose them and they choose us. We can define who we are with new friends, and we select who and when to be friends with different people based on our needs at that time. As you age, you choose your friends more selectively based on your own needs. For example, after school ends where proximity, common lifestyle, and time makes friendships easier, you realize that you actually need two different kinds of friends: 911 and 711.

911 friends are the ones you know will drop whatever they are doing to help you in an emergency. They will listen to you and fight for you. They will not chastise you for being too busy to call. They understand you better than others, so they allow you to be yourself but will also tell you gently when you are out of line. More than likely, you have only a small number of these kinds of friends. They are the water in your life that is as important as the air provided by a solid family. 911 friends and family fill up your Maslovian third level with love and belonging.

When asked how many social media (Facebook, LinkedIn, Twitter, etc.) 'friends' women had, answers ranged from zero to several thousand.

When asked how many "real friends" the women had (as in the type of friends that would really help out in a significant, self-less way when needed), the numbers were also all over. Some reported having a small handful, while others claimed to have dozens of loyal, reliable friendships.

The only exception to these findings was with women over 60. While most have the same number of social media friends, they reported usually a very small number, such as two or three, really good friends.

Do we get more selective, or are we too busy to foster friendship as we age?

Need someone to pick up little Johnny after school so you can run an errand? Want to share some laughs with a girlfriend over cosmos? Need a shoulder to cry on, a good babysitter referral or a drive-time phone pal? You have some 711 friends for these moments. Like the store 7-Eleven®, a 711 friendship is for convenience. They can often fill your needs, but only within the boundaries of their own priorities. They are quite helpful and you are grateful for their friendship. They will visit you in the hospital, bring food and balloons, but probably won't stay for long periods of time because they have other priorities. They will come to your mother's funeral if it's local, but wouldn't fly there to make it. They are necessary parts of your life puzzle, and they help fill your need to belong quite well most of the time. Just make sure you have some balance. Don't forget about your 911 gems. Keep some of those relationships in good shape for life's inevitable emergencies.

### Assets or Liabilities?

You probably even have friends that you would consider liabilities. These are takers and not givers. They take your time, emotional energy and maybe even your confidence. You know, those women that are so insecure about themselves that they position themselves so you feel lucky to be their friends — when, in reality, it's the other way around. These are women who go out of their way to tell you where they shop, what they wear and who they date without asking you anything about your own life. These are the women who clearly judge you without knowledge and tell you about other people that you should avoid. They are the first to criticize others and the last to compliment anyone.

So why the heck are we friends with them? Because we are needy, too. We may find comfort in their outward 'pathetic-ness'. We may truly believe they really need us and aren't as bad as they seem. However, if you were a guy, you know you would have cut them loose a long time ago. Instead, we put up and shut up and wonder why they continue to take advantage of us. So who's more pathetic?

It's easy to advise you to stop investing more in a friend or family member who is a liability. But, seriously, stop going out of your way to be nice and helpful to them and then feeling badly that they don't reciprocate. Be cordial if you must maintain the relationship but don't feel badly about leaving it at that. You have limited time and energy so spend it with people who matter and who appreciate you. If you ran your life like a business, you would have fired those bad friends a long time ago, focused on your assets, and moved on. Not such a bad idea... do you agree?

## People Don't Change as Much as Your Needs Do

With time, your personal needs, and subsequently your friends, will change. You find yourself spending more time with friends who have kids of similar age and gender. Perhaps your neighbors are now your hangout friends simply because they are nearby. You'll have gym friends, bus stop buddies and even work pals — but if you were 20 again and had the time and ability to choose your friends more actively, most of the people you have on your holiday card list probably wouldn't be on it.

You may no longer need a manicure buddy but rather a bridge partner. You need someone who understands what it's like to be 40 and unmarried or 50 without ever having kids. You need someone who's dealt with a sick older parent or a disabled child. You need friends with common life experiences and needs. And this means some of the old entourage isn't quite working well for you anymore.

Friendships will change over time. Some 911 friends will become 711 friends and vice versa. Some new ones will join your personal community and others will leave. Some will disappoint you while others will surprise you. Just realize this is normal and part of the journey. For women compared to men, it seems very easy to make both kinds of friends. But actually, as we get older, we accumulate a lot of acquaintances (not even 711 friends) which take up our time and energy too. As a result, it gets harder to keep 911 friendships strong on both sides of the relationship. As we age, we get stuck in our ways. Therefore, we become pickier. We may be cordial to many but genuinely interested in only a few. And the more we age, the more we find ourselves happy to be restrictive, if not alone.

The Internet makes this all worse, too. Besides from wasting time that we could use otherwise to build deep relationships, we now have the ability to have many shallow friendships and connections. With social media, intended or not, we are a persona that is different than who we really are. Our profiles are only an approved snapshot of what we decide to post. Online you can be anyone you want to be and subsequently be friends with anyone who likes that persona you've created.

Plus, we all know that having hundreds of Facebook, Twitter or even LinkedIn friends isn't a sign of popularity but usually one of propaganda. Sociologists have proven that humans can only have beneficial relationships with about 300 people and meaningful ones with only a handful. Needless to say, many people judge their worth by their online connections and their seeming following. It's not really a surprise that over 80% of Twitter posts never get read. A religious zealot has a better chance of being heard standing on a wooden soapbox in Times Square.

If you are excited to find high school friends from 30 years ago, question why it took so long if they meant that much to you. It's indeed fun to find out what they are doing — perhaps even comforting to hear that most everyone ended up just like you or worse off. What about finding old boyfriends who dumped you that are now bald and fat with ugly kids? Absolutely fantastic! Maybe it's even entertaining to hear all the old gossip you never heard back then like who was doing what and to whom. But are these online relationships real and do they make you a better person? I'll leave answering that question up to you. Suffice it to say, when there is a will, there is always a way — with or without Facebook.

Here is one last consideration about the people who are your life cast and how you play it all out. When someone doesn't pay back a favor or compliment, don't wince. Take it as data towards better managing your life's balance sheet in gaining the right mix of friends and family members that really make your life better for you. I am not implying to get even, but rather realize that everyone has Maslovian motives and needs. The more you can 'normalize' other people's bone-head behavior, the better you can cope with it and move on. Maybe one day, it really will just roll off your back. Meanwhile, at least know it's not you. It's them and their uncontrollable need to feel better about themselves.

## Girl Talk Guidelines

1. Has anyone you cared about responded negatively to an idea of yours that you shared that you thought was great? How did that make you feel? Why do you think that person reacted negatively?

2. How many social media friends do you have and actively engage with and why?

3. How much time do you estimate spending on social media and other personal electronic communication (e.g. Text, Skype, email, etc.) per day? Is this good or bad? Do you think you should spend more or less?

4. How do you think social media is going to change the nature of relationships in the future? How do you see it impacting different generations now?

# Ms. matched

Bad boys can be good for you

> 62.5% of women surveyed said they dated someone who was clearly not a good guy — someone who was handsome, rich, and/or gregarious but clearly superficial and not genuinely caring.
>
> One woman commented, "Who hasn't?"

Mental masochism. Maybe even mental masturbation. It makes us feel good. More precisely, it massages our "egas" (female ego). Dating a guy who we know is not a good person but looks good is really a turn-on. We are attracted to these types like bears to honey. We want them to want us. We want others to admire us because of it. We want to prove to ourselves that we are equally attractive, yet we know these relationships are not going to end well. We know he will do something that will inevitably break our heart or at least sting us with a harsh reality check.

Why do we want to be with these bad boys? Because we like the attention we get from other people. Whether envy from other women, jealousy from another man, or even the berating we get from friends and family — it's all wanted attention. When they break our hearts, we feel twice as ashamed since we think people are reveling saying, "I told you so."

But, in the end, we all know we go for the bad boys because they do make us feel good. They make us feel a sense of…belonging. It's belonging to something that gives us confidence, social interest and popularity. However, it's not about belonging to something that has true personal value. He has value to you and by dating him you want to believe that you bring value to him. At least you hope so. You hope you both bring to one another more than arm candy and the comment, "You look so cute together." Do you enjoy one another's company when you are without other people around? Do you have fun together as well as fun apart? Do you give each other your best and worst physical and emotional presence? Do you really like the person, or do you like yourself with that person?

When you are in your twenties, it's hard to know the answers to these questions because you really don't know yourself yet. We play a mean game of musical chairs trying to find the best possible mate to grab and "settle down with." While we'll specifically talk more about marriage later on in the book, it's interesting to note here that 30% of our surveyed women had been married more than once. And even with these additional chances to get the perfect mate, 20% still said they would change their husband if they could do so easily. This didn't mean they were getting a divorce but rather that if they could rewind and take a do-over, they would make a different choice.

### Relationships Are Like Underwear

When you talk to people who have been married more than once and who are now in satisfying marriages, you usually find a common reason for the failure of their initial marriage. They admit to not really knowing the person they married the first time and then found out a whole bunch of things about their spouses that were devastating surprises. Things like their husbands were terrible at handling crises, or that their husbands listen to their mother's advice and none other.

A few noted that their husbands couldn't hold down a job and some said their husbands never changed while they both grew older.

So with the wisdom of first marriages, and being older themselves, these women acknowledge that relationships are analogous to underwear. The older and more experienced you get, the thongs and other outwardly sexy under garments get replaced by more functional, practical wares. When you don't even really see someone's underwear after a while, you realize the underwear is not important but that other things are — the body, the touch, the technique, the intent.

Relationships are the same. Initially, the outside is what seems interesting, but over time, your other senses need input. A pretty, but incompatible boy just won't finish the race. We know that, but yet try to run with these boys anyway, at least while we are young or just want to feel young.

## What We Really Want is an Advocate

I believe there are three major "a-ha's" in life:

1. Your parents are human and therefore can be wrong.
2. You need to know and play by someone else's rules before you get to create your own.
3. We all want a personal advocate.

You may be a very strong, smart woman who is aggressive and decisive. But no matter how well we take life by the horns and 'steer' it in our own direction, we still want someone to be there to do it for us, at least once in a while. I don't mean a side-kick or Driver's Ed instructor with a second wheel. I mean someone who literally takes the wheel and drives for us (anyone humming Carrie Underwood?). That driver makes us feel empowered and allows us to drive when we want, but they are there to take control when we lose it, can't or don't want to handle it. They are there to reinforce our decisions or even to make them for us. They are there to kick our butts when we feel unworthy.

We want people in our lives that make us go to the doctor when we should and if it comes to it, they will hunt down the doctor to tend to us if we can't do that on our own.

We need a shoulder to cry on, but more a shoulder to lean on. We need someone who will fight for us, who will defend us and who will let us be a princess once in a while. Perhaps fairy tale fed, this is a real human need and, of course, tied to our Maslovian need to belong.

Admit it girls, we want a "real man" (even if it's in the form of another woman) who will take care of us. We can deny it and deal with it. But in the end, we still want it. It's just the way we are wired. It's not to say men don't need tending to as well. They do. It's just as modern women have gotten stronger and more independent, both men and women assume that women don't want this coddling as much. I think in many ways we need it more. We make decisions for our families, for our businesses, associations, clubs, etc. With all that consideration, it can be quite comforting to have someone who can make decisions about us, for us. And while a business coach, a shrink, a consultant or even a book can help, in the end, day-to-day life advocacy is best when it comes out of love, not out of pocket.

## Girl Talk Guidelines

1. Recall a bad boy relationship you had/have and why you were/are attracted to him.

2. How have your relationship priorities changed over time? How do you expect them to change in the future?

3. Do you have a life advocate? Who is it and why? Who is theirs? Are you a life advocate for someone else?

4. If you could re-do your romantic relationships again, how would you do things differently?

# Ms. Fortune

## In sickness and in wealth

*40% of Americans think marriage is obsolete*

— Pew Research Center

You may already be outraged by the chapter title and above statistic. You have every right. However, if you've been married for more than a few years, chances are that you relate to the fact that marriage is not quite the deal you were sold. People say marriage takes work and that it's something sacred. By now, I hope you can easily see how marriage is also part of our Maslovian need to belong to another human being and family unit.

Marriage helps us fit in socially and avoid the stigmas associated with being unattached (not belonging). Despite the shifts in society of more and more unwed mothers and divorce as something common, heterosexual (and perhaps pervasively soon homosexual) marriage holds a critical place in our hierarchy of needs that allows us to feel secure and 'normal' relative to the world around us.

42% of married women in our survey claimed they had sex with their spouse 4-8 times per month. About a third of all respondents said they have sex with their spouses 2-3 times each month and 16% have sex less than once per month.

However, there are many things that no one tells you about marriage. Beyond the inevitable stress of bringing two families together before, during and after a wedding, marriage also represents a melding of habits, traditions, and values that aren't always apparent prior to marriage, or even in the first few years. Sure, you can live with someone to see if he is a slob or how often his mother calls — but, you don't know someone will change as time marches on, bringing all sorts of unplanned challenges and opportunities. These are the things that morph relationships and subsequently impact marriages.

## You Can't Ignore Boring or Snoring

What most people won't tell you is that marriage over time is actually quite boring. You wake up and go to sleep with the same person day after day. He snores and makes you tired and cranky. He loses his hair, which rarely makes him sexier. You both gain weight and 'earn' wrinkles that really aren't all that rewarding. You see each other at your worse — sick, tired, uncoiffed.

After years of the same predictable chatter, you no longer really pay attention or care about the details of his workday and you try to share your own in an interesting way. But the truth is, your day lives are separate and your night lives sparse. You get tired by 9 pm and the ideal night is one home in comfy (a.k.a. ugly) PJs curled up with a glass of wine living vicariously by reading People magazine. Going to the movies is just too much hassle and eating out is great when you have others to keep conversation happening. When you are alone together, you talk about the kids, the house, the relatives and other relatively mundane issues but you rarely, if ever, talk about why you aren't sexually aroused by him or that you haven't had sex together in weeks. Fact is, few couples have sex with each other regularly and, more interestingly, many are having sex secretly with other people. Stop blushing. Yeah, it's true. Sex is at the bottom of Maslow's Hierarchy and therefore it's a human need, not just desire. If it's not getting fulfilled by hubby, then often nature provokes us to find other ways to get it…as in affairs, toys, or both. Face it: no one is that engaging to keep the same fire burning forever. Even the Olympic Flame needs a change of venue every four years.

> 40.5% of our married respondents said they or someone they knew was having an extramarital affair. Only 15.4% of the 20-29 year olds said they have even considered it. 30% of the 50-59 year olds said they have or know someone who has had an affair and 40% of the 60+ year olds did!
>
> However, almost making the numbers above questionably low, 83.1% of the women said they or another woman that they know has had sex with a married man (assuming it's not a fixed number of women having all those trysts)!

Whether it's a fling or a long-term arrangement, finding a partner outside of a marriage is still taboo and can be significantly dangerous to the marriage and everything around it. However, in many cases, it may be what's keeping a marriage together. With the lustful honeymoon over, many couples find their union is one of convenience and choreographed function. One makes the lunches, the other coaches kids' soccer. One pays the bills, the other buys the groceries. We create little life plays that script our roles and characters. Eventually the play gets routine. Then we try to spice it up, seek counseling or try to do more together to bring new scenes into the performance. But the surprises are gone knowing how he will react and what he will do. Romance may still be used on each other, but now is more an acknowledgement that you are still together — even without the same lustful desire. It's not that the magic is gone, it's just that you now know all the tricks.

Some women will simply adjust to this and focus on other things like their children, their jobs, hobbies, or other activities. It's hard to think of knitting or Bunco as filling a sexual void. But with moral boundaries preventing a more exact substitute, safe and productive distractions are common choices.

### He's Gay and She's Blissfully Ignorant

Perhaps you are on your second or third marriage trying to find someone that will keep the candle lit for longer than a few years. It's rather typical that first marriages don't work out simply because the couple outgrows one another or really couldn't see the truth through the veil of youthful lust.

Do you know of a couple that is still full of sexual energy around one another that has been together for more than a year? It's rare. Though I bet you know a couple that is seemingly happy but you definitely suspect that one of the individuals is gay. They seem comfortable and compatible and you are amazed and amused that one or both don't acknowledge the issue. 50% or more of our respondent groups acknowledged they knew such a couple. Can you imagine having a partner that plays his husbandly role really well but doesn't need your sexual attention? Are you relieved by that? Many women admitted that sounded like utopia.

### Marriage Requires a Contract

Many women will admit that marriage is quite literally a financial shelter for them (yes, Maslow levels 1 and 2). Whether they or their spouses are the breadwinners, marriage is like a small business that has credits and debits, managers and employees. It has rules, even if unwritten, and it has operational expectations. And just like a business where "he who controls the spending controls the company", in a marriage, he or she who earns the most controls the marriage. This means that there is a non-negotiable, inherent rule that whoever brings home the bacon gets to ultimately decide when, how and with whom it will be eaten. The woman may control the checkbook, the debit cards and other spending vehicles; but if the husband earns and provides for the family, he most likely ultimately maintains the alpha position in the pack. It may be subtle and not noticeable to anyone outside (or even acknowledged inside) the marriage, but it's still there. He or she, wh ever earns the money, wears the proverbial pants and maintains silent, but powerful, veto power.

> 25% of women under the age of 60 would not choose their husbands again if they could go back and change.

### Happiness is Spending Someone Else's Money When You Don't Have To

Therefore, as the chapter title implies, marriage is as much about financial security as it is about sexual and social belonging. My friend Susan Joyce, founder of job-hunt.org, stated to me once, "My happiness is usually measured by the amount in my savings account." I have to agree with her in most every way. I would complement that with a corollary thought: "Utter happiness is spending someone else's money when you don't have to." This implies that when there is true financial freedom, the personal power is level. And, therefore, there is pleasure in having someone treat you not out of need but out of desire.

Consider how much nicer it is when you buy someone like your husband/partner a gift with your money and not his/hers. Get a part-time job, sell some things on eBay, or even ask your husband for an allowance if it helps you to build a small nest egg that you can use to buy things on your own terms. And if you are the breadwinner, tell your husband to do the same. Diamonds are a girl's best friend when they are bought with someone else's money and without strings or the price tag attached.

Therefore, don't let a lack of money dictate how you interact with others or how they interact with you. You don't need millions. You just need the comfort to feel you can do and buy things that would make you or others happy, even slightly. Having that ability is powerful and will subsequently allow some balance of power and make all your relationships stronger, including your marriage.

## Girl Talk Guidelines

1. Why did you marry your husband? If you are still married, why do you stay married?

2. If you could go back and change your decision to marry, would you and why?

3. What advice would you give to someone who is getting married for the first time?

4. When you have sex with your husband, are you fantasizing about someone else? Is this bad?

# Ms. stress

## We were born XX rated

By now you know that sex is not a luxury but rather something Maslow says we need in order to thrive. Our creativity and self-actualization depends on it! You also know that boring and snoring is symptomatic of getting beyond the honeymoon and growing older with someone who is, after all, just human. Lastly, you also know now that life is tough and full of challenges that you can at best minimize with the right luck, money and foresight.

*So here's the truth once again. Sex is a defining part of a woman's life cycle.*

As teenagers, our hormones are raging. This new experience is like trying wine for the first time. You aren't sure you necessarily like it, but you want to try more. You hear it is great and it feels at least interesting, so you do more and then find eventually that it's really good. You know the risks, but that's half the fun.

So now into your twenties you are worried about what to be when you really grow up. You go to college or have other opportunities to live away from home which allows you, theoretically, to have sex anytime. Maybe you explore as much as you can with the limitations of what your morality and the available partners enable you to do. More than likely, you experiment with different types of sex and your M.O. is to go from class or work to social outings/parties and back to work/class — one funding the other with entertainment and goals. At around 25 or so, you start to think about finding "the one" and while you still may be enjoying the freedom, you know in the back of your mind that you need to at least start looking.

By thirty, you are attached, married or worried. You need to find a mate and you get more neurotic every time a friend gets engaged or announces her pregnancy. As the musical mating game continues, you hope to find the one person that you are convinced is "yours". You don't want to be the one left without the seat and the concern of family and friends with thinking that you are defective.

If you marry, sex with your spouse brings comfort and true belonging. But…then come babies and you are relieved to let people know that you are fertile and have been 'chosen' to parent a child. You experience great joy along with excitement and fear, extreme belonging and responsibility.

What you don't expect is that you no longer really want to have sex. You tell your spouse that you are uncomfortable or that you have other physical limitations. However, in reality, pregnancy actually gives you a convenient excuse to gratefully avoid sex. You just don't want to get messy. And any amount of sleep is more enticing than anything that involves physical effort — and this just gets worse after the baby comes.

Sleeplessness is bad for a lot of things like driving, being civil and definitely for maintaining an active sex life. Now, when you are lying down, you actually want to be left alone. My friend Angela quipped during her divorce proceedings that she didn't see any fine print in her marriage license that required her to do laundry or give blow jobs. After a few years of marriage and rearing kids, sex often becomes an obligation and almost a contractual requirement …at least until you turn 45.

**Perio is the Muse of Mistresses**

Sure, you expect your eyesight to wane and other body parts to gradually surrender to gravity. We see enough advertising to remind us about our changing maturing figures and our need to poison the crows with Botox because they left unsightly footprints (aka crow's feet or wrinkles) around our eyes. But then all of a sudden, as if it were only going to happen to your mother and other older women, your gynecologist all of a sudden talks to you about "the change". As if it's something you need to know about! And then, because she said the "m" word, you begin hearing and seeing information about it all over. It's like you have new radar that detects all of this otherwise subliminal menopausal content. Its nuts — your friends, magazines, your fitness trainer — all seem to be pinging you with talk about menopause. And perhaps in spite of that, or because of that, you become crazy horny. It's as if you are again 20 and just can't help but secretly ogle sexy, young men. Those "he's young enough to be my son" boys all look hot — even if they are your son's friends. You can easily justify Mrs. Robinson by realizing that she wasn't really a bad influence but rather she was a charitable educator. After all, young men should all be that lucky to experience an older woman. Demi Moore may just be our generational role model. Half (Demi) her age means she gets more (Moore)!?

**Libido is FDA Approved**

As noted previously, 40% of our married survey respondents admitted that they or someone they knew was having an extramarital affair, and 83% of unmarried respondents had sex with a married man. Are you disgusted or wondering how to get in on that action?

With so many people doing it, the obvious question is: "Is extramarital sex so bad"? If a marriage has become one of mutual convenience, how does the need for sex get dealt with? If the partners don't want or can't have sex with one another, is it, in fact, good to have sex with someone else to relieve that marital 'tension'? Is guilt-free sex enough to satisfy both partners' need for lustful, 'personally being desired' (belonging) sex?

The rub here is that women can't just have sex. We typically need to have or create emotional attachment and that is where we inevitably can't consummate anything with 'no strings attached'. If we could just have sex like Samantha on "Sex in the City", would we be better wives to our husbands? That goes unanswered for many women because they don't let themselves go there due to morals, religion or other barriers that teach us "thou shall not kill or screw they neighbor". Wouldn't it be great if the Bible told us to exercise regularly and have sex for our mental and physical well-being? Can you imagine classes like "Pray, Pump and Hump", "Confess, Stretch and Spread"?...hmmmm...

We are left with the dilemma of dealing with our newfound forties sexual prowess and the knowledge that our marriage just ain't helping. Whether we reach out and physically touch someone or utilize the high-tech alternatives such as sexting and video sex, it's no wonder that the fastest growing population of online users is 40+ women! Facebook friends, yeah sure...

It doesn't seem right either that our male counterparts look like hell. They are for the most part bald, fat and all together do look like my father's Oldsmobile! Meanwhile, us ladies, we look great. We are all dressed up but have nowhere to go or any way to get laid — or so it seems. We just don't brag about this accomplishment very often. But according to our survey, that doesn't mean it's not happening often.

Notice a co-worker or a friend with the new glow? She's either trying to get some action or already is. She may be married, but she's not dead. She's just fulfilling her Maslovian quest and building the foundation of her pyramid so she can be a better person. (Bet you never thought of it that way!)

### Make No Mystique About It

Now doesn't that make you feel better? I just gave you permission to have unadulterated, albeit safe, sex with your husband, your hand, a toy or, even if you want, with someone else! Well, that is only if you can handle it. If you must be emotionally involved, don't do it. If you will have guilt and regret, please don't even consider it. If you have religious or moral concerns, then be true to what you believe. However, if you are sexually frustrated and not having sex because you are married and think no one else is, get over that. They are and perhaps you should too.

However, I will make a strong note here that several people that I personally know who ventured outside of their marriage to enjoy sex with another partner have been very burned. That is, their husbands ultimately did find out and, in some cases, this blew up their marriages and overall family ties. Children were permanently scarred and friends parted. Therefore, I am not advocating having extramarital sex without serious consideration of the ramifications to your mental well-being as well as to those important to you. In fact, I am amazed at how many smart women lose their intelligence when they start an affair, even if it's not yet physical. We joke that men think with their penises. I think a 40+ year-old woman thinks with her hormones. Yes, your husband can see that you texted somebody else's number 1000 times last month. Yes, he notices that you are dolling up just to run to the grocery store. Yes, he notices you cringe when he touches you even in the slightest, non-sexual way. So be smart, be careful and, most importantly, be true to what you really need and want.

Take a moment to figure out why you want to have extramarital sex and then decide if it is really in the best interest for you personally and if you can live with the possible implications. I guess I wasn't surprised that in this area on our survey a few women noted they swing with their husbands, and they don't consider that extr marital sex. It's a way for them both to fulfill their sexual needs 'consensually' while acknowledging they need something more than what their spouse can deliver.

Bet your mamma never told you that!

Life is indeed challenging enough with things we can't control and things we just can't predict. Needing sex and getting it are both predictable and controllable. So why not deal with that and make room for the other things that need our energy and attention? Your car needs oil changes to run efficiently. You need sex so you can, too. Vroom, vroom.

## Girl Talk Guidelines

1. Are you shy talking about sex and sexual things with your partner? With others? Why?

2. Do you enjoy sex for yourself or do you do it more for the other person?

3. If you considered having an affair (outside your own marriage or with someone who is married), why? Why not?

4. How did you or would you react if a friend said she was having an extramarital affair or a relationship with someone married?

# Ms.conceived

## Motherhoodwinked

"Your life is about to change in ways you can't imagine." Boy oh boy, girl oh girl, that is the biggest understatement of every pregnant woman. Change? How about redirected? Sabotaged? Overtaken?

As if the effects of pregnancy were not enough, children themselves take over your life in a way that defies profoundness. Your attention is focused, your interests reigned and your non-essential time and money are all but spent. The exchange: a crying, pooping, vomiting little person who you obsess about morning and night.

When you finally wake up from your post-partum sleep deprivation coma, you realize motherhood is a ton of work including laundry, feeding, cleaning and planning. You also find out that the baby is not even the most demanding individual but rather your friends, other mothers, your own mother and your spouse/partner's mother are the real challenge. Whether they tell you outright how to be a better mother, they can't help themselves in passing judgment and trying to be helpful. Well intended or not, you are the lucky recipient of motherly advice from everyone else who ever had a child — even if their own child is now a convicted serial killer.

Circumcise? Private school? Vaccinate? Plastic bottles? Disposable diapers? Organic? Too much TV? Too little reading? Video games? The Internet? Soccer or baseball? Spanish or Chinese? Drugs? Girls? Boys? Cults? Facebook? College? Job? Marriage? Oy!

### The Noblest Cause of All

What could be more significant than giving birth and molding someone's life? To this great honor and responsibility, there is a maternal sisterhood. We 'get' each other. We may share the experiences of showcasing our cervix to a maternity ward full of passersby, flashing an occasional boob while trying to get the baby latched on in an otherwise public place, and the all too common question whether your child really is yours since he/she looks nothing like you. ("Is it possible the nurse made a mistake?")

But in all seriousness, motherhood can be the most significant part of a woman's life. It gives us a sense of accomplishment, of purpose and direction. Most definitely it gives us something that belongs to us and that we belong to. "I am a mom, therefore I am."

Pretty much across age groups, mothers ages 20-60+ said their children's health was their primary concern. A distant second was safety. 3rd, 4th, 5th were academic achievement, being social with lots of friends or at least not picked on, and then being well-dressed.

Athletic ability ranked lowest except with moms ages 30-39 who cared much more about their little athletes while they didn't care as much as other moms about how their kids dressed. Young moms were less concerned about academic achievement for their children than older moms, but the young moms felt a higher need to keep their kids safe.

There are many somewhat obvious things such as safety, education, health and social compatibility that are all part of parenting. They are challenging no matter how well educated or affluent you are. We get measured on these things through the child's schooling and interaction with other children. Play dates become quasi-focus groups to ensure acceptable social development. College applications ultimately measure our kids (and our?) academic and related accomplishments. These things are relatively predictable. However, many people don't anticipate as parents that there are two relatively selfish effects: first, your desire to be better than other parents; and second, the desire to be better than your own parents.

## Crocs, Crock Pots and Other Parenting Crap

Even if you don't consider yourself to be a brand-influenced dresser, you will be more attentive to children's products. Whether it's buying the 'best' car seat or organic milk, you will find it easier to justify buying the more expensive options for your kids.

This doesn't mean you'll necessarily buy your kids Juicy Couture, but you will probably buy things they, or you, don't and won't ever need. ("We better have an epi pen in the house and an extra bottle of Tylenol just in case!") You never want your children to look like they need a haircut while you'll walk around with grey roots and tell yourself that no one will notice.

Perhaps the biggest surprise in motherhood is the guilt you feel in watching other mothers. The unwritten pressure to be PTO-proactive, gym-fit, socially-involved and, thereafter, a good wife and friend can, and is, overwhelming. Throw in that already over-boiling pot a job (if you work) and/or health issues and there is just no room in the soup for hobbies, shopping or other things that you do just for fun. Yeah, everyone has the same 24 hours, but when you are a mom, many of those hours are lopped off the top by your family. You also lose energy from the stress that comes with that responsibility. If you feel tired even after you sleep, you aren't alone.

So whether you worry about the right labels to dress your kids, or if you worry whether they have the right friends, the right extracurricular, the right teachers, the right teaching method, the right nutrition or the right attitude, you find out that having a baby is easy. Being a mom is unquestionably hard.

You hate saying "no" to your child who presents a reasonable but untimely request. You even hate saying "no" just because "you said so". More than anything, you hate saying no and hearing your own parents in the tone.

### Vicarious is Really "MyCurious"

The second motherhood surprise is your ongoing subconscious need to be a better parent than your own. You want to give your kids more and also have them appreciate you more than you did your parents. You want them to have opportunities that you never had, to have comforts you never enjoyed and, most urgently, you want them to always want you in their lives.

So I challenge you to think about this underlying need and consider the implications. Dragging them from one lesson to another, from a sports game and then to practice, is perhaps good exposure for them to find what they really like to do. However, we know that over-programming kids isn't good and, more importantly, aiming kids to do things you did or would have liked to do isn't much better. They won't really find things they like but rather things that make you feel good, which in turn, reflects a positive behavior cue to them. Just like training a dog that doesn't really want to sit or roll over. You give him a physical treat, such as a dog cookie, as well as reinforce his behavior by telling him he is a good dog. Perhaps we do this inadvertently with our children, too. When was the last time you opened up a catalog of courses and workshops and let your child pick the one he or she wanted? Did you ever urge your child to stick with something that he or she didn't like by convincing both of you that more time was needed to get better at it? What about bragging to other parents about your child's success on the field or in the studio? We all do that and don't realize it's our way of assuming some of that glory — after all, we gave birth to that protégé! Since he/she carries your genes, it must be that you were never given the same chance, but now through your child you can experience what it would have been like.

Not only is this probably not good for your kid, it can be very hard for you when your child doesn't want or can't continue to shine. That's a lot of pressure for everyone. Call me the anti-Tiger Mom. I just believe that childhood only happens once and it should be filled with happy memories. If I could play God for one day, I would wish that everyone would have a happy childhood, feeling loved and appreciated. I bet there would be more room in our prisons and less stress in our lives.

> 31.2% of our surveyed women said they remember having an unhappy childhood. Our sample of women over 60 were even worse off with 66.7% reporting unhappy childhood memories. Was this a reflection of tougher parenting style and custom? Was it more time to reflect and realize? We can't really tell.

### Choice is the Real Prize

So here's a real secret to parenting survival: many of your worries are unnecessary. Most people don't go to Harvard and yet do fine. Few people play professional baseball or do ballet — most don't do it at all as adults. Even fewer remember what they wore or who they played with as children with minimal detail or ramification.

As parents, we must worry about safety since a child or even a teenager can't yet. We must provide for them and we must be responsible for them to the rest of society. These are things that are non-negotiable. What we forget often, though, is that our role is not one of making them the smartest, most liked, or even most confident.

Our role is to provide them with the ability to have and make good choices. This means that when they become adults and can choose for themselves, they have minimal obstacles and maximum good sense. They are smart enough, popular enough, athletic enough, or otherwise talented enough to do what they really want. Being well-educated gives us more choices. Being well-liked enables us to have connections that ultimately help us get what we choose. We want them to be able to play on the company softball team without embarrassment. We may want them to be good enough to sing in the church choir. We may want them to earn a living painting, teaching, selling, sailing, cooking, judging or writing! Since those things aren't predetermined at birth, as a parent, we try to give our children the chance to be and do anything they choose without the limits of a childhood deprived of potential and experiences. We want to open all the doors and let them follow their dreams. We want to enable them through guided exposure and empower them through vicarious enthusiasm.

Where this gets limited is with how much you can afford to do and how well both you and your child are willing to experiment. If your child wants to ski though no one else in the family knows how, will you let her? If you child is not musical while everyone else around him is, how will that play out? If you know your child is extraordinarily smart but lazy, will you allow her to be average? These are all things that in the big scope of life that may not really matter. What seems to matter in the end is having a choice. When you have choices, you have freedom and you have power. With choice, you have the ultimate currency and can obtain what is of value to you. With choice, your children will have happiness. The world is their oyster.

At least this is theoretically true. Unfortunately, many people grow up with too many choices and too little appreciation for them. Sheryl Crow reminds us, "It's not having what you want. It's wanting what you've got."

So how do we ground ourselves and our children to have a chance and choice for real happiness?

31.3% of our survey audience claimed they did not have a happy childhood. Most stated it was due to parents being uninvolved or too strict. These and many other deep-seated reasons make us want to be better than our own parents and the best parent, period. Whether we actually act on this wish is a different story. The desire to be a great parent is pretty pervasive. And while we know we don't want to be like our own mother, we can't help ourselves. It isn't until we realize that we are the best parent we can be, that we also realize that most likely our mother was the same. There is no school, no certificate, no degree, not even a test you can take to prove you are a great parent. So remember that you can be as good of a mother as you define it for yourself — even beyond how it was taught to you.

This brings us back to Maslow and the criticality of belonging. Obtaining a sense of belonging starts at birth and at home. It's inevitably determined by a mother's (and/or father/partner/other adult's) love and attention. It continues through childhood into adulthood such that grown women forever bemoan the impact of their mother's words or actions and how they negatively impact the confidence and decisions they make even as adults. Often, when I talk to women even over 60, they tell me they are forever haunted by their mother's doubt and negative feedback. So I extrapolate from another profound lyric. This one is from John Mayer: "Mothers be good to your daughters. And Mothers be good to your sons, too."

## Girl Talk Guidelines

1. What do you think constitutes a good and healthy childhood?

2. Do you consider yourself to be a better parent than your own? How so?

3. What are the most important things you want your children to know and do?

4. Who was influential to you growing up? Why?

# Ms. guided

## Mentor starts with men

"Find thee a mentor."

I've been told this many times in leadership and other self-improvement classes. Find someone who inspires you and has the success you desire. Find someone that will take you under his or her wing and teach you the written and unwritten rules. Sounds great! Where do I find one? More importantly, where do I find one that is female?

With regard to work, we see business schools being filled with a majority of women. Therefore, we would expect to see more in the boardrooms and in management overall. However, that's not really helping to provide more female mentors because one of two scenarios is happening. EITHER the career-serious woman is fighting for that elite position among her male peers and as such isn't interested in letting in any female competition. OR, she is managing her work with the rest of her chaotic world with family and social needs which means she's just too damn busy to stop and help a junior dame.

Maybe those are not comforting excuses, but they are true. So here's the good news: men are not only more plentiful as mentors, they can be better. Look for the ones that don't feel threatened by a woman and can actually get brownie points for such an effort. Corporate kudos will come to them by helping out the little gals, but also from their peers who may see it as a macho, upper classmen thing to do.

For you, if you pick a good mentor, you gain the inside view from his privileged perspective. He won't worry about the small stuff, nor let you. A good mentor will steer you away from danger and towards political safety without all the petty considerations of who said what to whom. As you know, women aren't usually that calm.

## Complement. Don't Compete.

It's important to pick a mentor that has complementary skills to your own. In other words, don't compete with his talent, but rather bolster it with things that you can do that make HIM look better. If he's not a great writer but you are, offer to help edit memos or documents. If you are a great PowerPoint designer, offer to help him with that. If you enjoy research, see if you can provide him background info for important meetings or other things that will make him look smart and prepared. No, I am not telling you to be a 1960's style secretary à la "Mad Men". Rather, realize life is all about tit for tat (more so than we want to admit). In light of not giving actual tit (I am not recommending that because of longer term implications that I hope you don't want to deal with…), consider your mentor's motivation to help you. Does he need to feel important; and, therefore, will your request for mentoring make him feel empowered? Great! It should. But also know that over time, when the honor is replaced by effort, he needs to feel he is getting something out of the deal. He may get positive reinforcement from you and the organization, which is great. However, if you find things to help and complement his skill set, that is something worthwhile to him. And subsequently he will invest more in you.

Can you do that for a woman too? Certainly. However, as we know, women are naturally protective and potentially suspicious of any unsolicited help. Women managers can be like den mothers and may not let you into their caves to help tend to their cubs. I am not suggesting that you avoid all female mentors. I am suggesting that you keep your options open and really understand the person's (man or woman) Maslovian motivation for wanting to mentor you. Be sure that it's a win-win for both sides that is clearly understood by both of you. Like it or not, it's still a man's world and they get to make and keep a lot of rules that favor them. But, as in the overall game of life, knowing the rules and developing appropriate strategies will help you win and succeed. Getting a male mentor can be an invaluable shortcut and help. ('Manopoly' anyone?)

*"You've got to go out on a limb sometimes because that is where the fruit is."*

—Will Rogers

**You Are What You Wear**

Ines Sainz, a former Miss Universe turned TV sportscaster, created a frenzy when she showed up at a New York Jets practice in a low-cut blouse and tight jeans. Some criticized the Jets players for acting boorish while others noted that Sainz was "asking for it". MSNBC.com's Eve Tahmincioglu noted in her coverage, "Men can hide behind standard-issue suits, business casual or work clothes. No matter what they do, women get classified by their clothes. If they wear pantsuits or below-the-knee dresses, like Hillary Clinton or Janet Reno, men mock them as frumps or cold bitches. If they're deemed 'too sexy', like Sainz, CNBC's Maria Bartiromo, or Sarah Palin, men belittle them, too. So what the heck is appropriate female work attire? Every day, as we women pick out our outfits, we know we're walking a very fine line."

Once again, I note to you: reader beware. You are not going to like what I write here but it's (as always) honest and true. You are what you wear. Walk into any meeting and it's usually quite easy to see from people's clothing and posture who's in charge. This is even more pronounced with women. Women in upper ranks dress with more care and style. They don't always wear the top designers but they are careful to coordinate and accessorize well and seemingly spend time and money to look put together. This is a subtle but perhaps telling sign that they really are 'together' and can therefore lead others (directly or indirectly). And, of course, I am generalizing once again but from the vast majority of experiences I have had with groups at various companies in various industries, this is visibly true. You can pick out the people in charge simply by what they are wearing. Artists, construction workers, software developers, even stay-at-home moms — it doesn't matter. Your choice of clothes says a lot about you and your confidence.

Having many image consultants as clients, I have learned a lot about the fashion and image business. While I won't even try to teach that here with respect to the professionals that really do know this much better than I, let me summarize the concept of image consulting. If you aren't comfortable in your own skin, that is a bigger issue and often hard to fix. However, if you aren't comfortable in your clothes (for whatever reason), this is also easily visible to others and impacts the way they will think about and respond to you. Why do so many of us continue to be Ms. Fits when we can easily fix our clothes and make an amazing difference with our confidence and what we subsequently tell the world? Consider it superficial or not — clothes do make the man and they make the woman, too. What is your wardrobe saying about you?

This brings me back to the topic of men and mentors. Ask another woman about your clothes and she'll tell you that you either look great (doesn't want you to be mad at her) or that something specific isn't right (as in, "it's my duty to tell you since you asked"). This can be helpful but what you really want to know is, "Do I look good to the people that matter?" To get that real answer, ask someone in that category...your mentor.

Dress like a slut? No way! But dress to demonstrate confidence and care? Definitely. Those are the things that are attractive to everyone and will command presence, power and capability.

Is image everything? It can be in the absence of time. It allows others to make an instant and impactful impression before you get to say or do anything. Therefore, consider your image as important as your ability in the grand scheme of your desired success.

So what about outside of work? Does it really matter that you wear sweatpants before or after you're married? Hell, yeah. You know it as well as I do that when you dress to attract others, your partner will also be attracted, if not suspicious (which isn't always a bad thing). It is a long known fact that some women dress for other women while some dress for men. If you really want to make an impact, dress in a way that makes you feel confident and look together. This may mean sexy or just vibrant and creative. Whatever rocks your world — as long as you are consciously dressing in a way that conveys who you want to be.

> With the choices none, some, a lot or constantly preoccupied, 62% of the women surveyed indicated they only put some effort into the way they look. 34.4% said they put a lot. Only a handful of respondents did nothing or were constantly primping.

If you can't or don't want to get a professional image consultant's help, then ask your mentor…as in man. See what he thinks, really. Don't ask if you look fat. Ask him what he thinks of what you are wearing and look for the verbal and non-verbal signs. If he is smiling with happy eyes, you are in good shape. If he hesitates and says you look "fine", well, that is the feedback you need to adjust and try again.

Having a mentor is a great way to simply have a sounding board or validation that you clearly look and act appropriately so you can comfortably belong.

## Girl Talk Guidelines

1. What should a great mentor do for his/her mentee?

2. Who do you admire in your work environment? Why?

3. Who do you know dresses poorly? How so? Who dresses well? How so?

4. What do you think your clothes say about you?

# Ms.led

## Business starts and ends with BS

*When answering Entrepreneur's October 2010 question: "Is being your own boss too tough?"*

*One male respondent, Michael C. Podlesny stated, "Their loss…nothing makes you feel freer than being your own boss."*

*Female entrepreneur Latasha Selby confessed, "I had to wipe out all my negative thoughts with positive ones and realize my capabilities. Then I was able to get over my fear of financial independency…"*

*Alyssa asks, "Why is it that women have to apologize, justify and otherwise rationalize their worth?"*

We work for a variety of reasons. Most obviously, we work to make money. But some of us need to make money while others want to make money. Need is a relative term. Do you need to earn six-figures, or do you really want to earn that much so you can enjoy the spoils it affords you?

A recent study by Gallup and Healthways surveyed 450,000 Americans and found that an income of $75,000 or more allows people to feel money is not their main cause of unhappiness. In other words, people who earned less than $75K are unhappy mostly due to their concerns about money. People who earn more than that reported other things that top their list of what makes them happy. Money enables them to obtain many of those things. For example, having enough income to go out with friends or buy nice things can make you happy. If you can't afford to do that, you may or will probably be unhappy and apparently $75K is the cutoff point for finding that happiness. However, what the study also indicated is that, as one would imagine, money is tied to people's self-esteem and that earning more money helps boost confidence and a feeling of self-worth.

So no matter why you work, most likely there is an element of wanting to be valued, of having financial control and independence and, of course, wanting to belong.

### Commitment is Optional

> 25.5% of our respondents that work said they don't actually have to but want to. Women ages 40-49 were least required to work with 34% of the women in that group saying they opted to work while 91% of the 20-29 year olds said they had to work for financial survival.

Whether you work for yourself or for someone else, don't get all huffy over this next sentence. As women, we have the option not to work. Society allows us to find a partner to support us without shame or indignity. Men still don't really have that right. When a husband earns less than his wife, there are inevitable comments and issues they deal with that just don't fit the conventional gender mold. This doesn't mean it doesn't work or isn't acceptable; it's just not 'normal.'

My own household is like this and besides from the social pressure my very amazing husband does feel, I also feel social pressure to be more involved with my kids' schools and after school lives. I don't volunteer for as much charitable activity as I would like nor do I have much time for social activities that don't involve my kids. I work, therefore I am busy. But I admit that I work because I have to as the breadwinner, but also because it makes me feel good. I relish getting checks from happy clients and getting kudos after a presentation well-received. I look around often and remind myself that my well-educated and healthy children, safe home and comforting belongings are all worthwhile booty that I have amassed as a result of my life as a working woman.

But back to you. Whether you work because you need to or because you want to, society as a whole often doesn't think we need to. Really. There is an unsaid assumption that you are working because you choose to — either because you voluntarily picked the 'wrong' partner to support you or that you work to increase your household income beyond what is needed. With this assumption, two things happen. First, some people (men and women) won't take you seriously as a business person; and, second, you may not take yourself seriously.

I see this more pronounced with women entrepreneurs, particularly older ones. Women who start businesses are often (though by no means always) doing the business around something they enjoy and figure they can make money doing it. While this is a seemingly good thing in terms of job satisfaction, there is no separation of need and want. Doing something that you enjoy is usually by default something you will do only on your own terms, not necessarily the market's. This means when the going gets tough, many women entrepreneurs don't aggressively save their businesses. They don't go for venture capital and they don't do cold calling — in other words, they don't do whatever it takes to keep the business alive. They get busy with networking, social media, and even hire coaches, but they don't put their money where their mouths are simply because they are doing the work for love, not for survival.

Moreover, many women have someone supporting them so if their business fails, it's actually OK. It will hurt their egos, but it doesn't devastate their finances. Their husband (or other partner) figures it's a way to keep the budding entrepreneur happy so it's a relatively small expense and, who knows, it just may produce some revenue. Therefore, while most of these women will tell you they take their businesses very seriously, even if they do, others may not.

But alas, there are those business women who are truly serious about their careers. They pursue additional degrees and work to be as successful as they and their environment allow. I've done that and been there, too, and I definitely don't judge or criticize anyone for this determination. It's important to note, however, the societal opinion of working women is still that women have the option to work and this is applied to every woman regardless of her motivation or success in the workforce. And as long as there is a large population of stay-at-home moms, that option and opinion will always be available.

My aunt, a 1970's women's rights activist, once said to me that my generation and the ones that followed take these freedoms for granted. She said we have all our options now because of the women before us, and I don't disagree. I am not sure we take that for granted but rather that it opens up a host of other issues and challenges on who and what we can be.

The long known old boys' club rallies around their empathy that not working isn't a socially acceptable option for men. The club exists to share the burden of a society that gives them no option but to work and to prove their worth through their work. Women don't have to do that. We know it and so do they. As such, I am not so sure that it is a club I am eager to belong to.

We still are paid less than our male counterparts and that feels utterly unfair. However, maybe we could justify that gap at least in our own minds as the price for our freedom to choose to work or not. Maybe that helps make that paycheck difference slightly less frustrating. Consider that your female citizenship entitles you to belong to a club that enjoys more choice and less pressure to work. It doesn't negate that many of us still need to work for financial reasons, but perhaps it helps us understand why there will always be challenges in the workplace for women of all talents and motivations.

### The Real Scarlet Letter is "S"

In Hawthorne's *Scarlet Letter*, his protagonist is forced to don a scarlet 'A' to indicate her otherwise secretive transgression of adultery. Written in 1850, it still has relevance to our lives with regards to what we are allowed to do and what we can keep personal.

However, as the survey data has already exposed, while adultery is in fact rather common, it is still kept hush-hush except in swinger circles and other still secretive arrangements that allow partners to mutually and proudly wear an A.

The reasons I bring this up here in a business chapter is that as a tall woman (5'9"), I find another type of scarlet letter on some men: an 'S'. They also don't wear it proudly like a varsity letter because the 'S' stands for "short". They have no way to hide that fact with their lack of vertical presence which inevitably impacts their confidence. Referred to as a Napoleonic complex, short men (short in my tall opinion is a man under 5' 7"), often and inevitably feel inferior. They know that other people can't help but pass an opinion based on the man's lack of physical presence. As such, short men often try to make up for their lack of height with falsely inflated egos and seemingly overconfident attitudes — especially to tall women. They can be snarky and aggressive, outright mean or quietly undermining. It seems ridiculous, but please trust me, in my own experience, and in talking with many other tall women, short men are often like this.

So I present this information just as a simple warning to be on guard, be careful and be smart. Short men can't hide being short (unless they are in Hollywood) and that has an unfortunate effect on their ability to be truly confident and easy to deal with. In too many negative encounters where I used to fight fire with fire, now I feel sorry for short men because their confidence has been crushed by a very visible physical disability. Maybe, most significantly, there is also a rather obvious assumption that little men have little parts too. *No grown man wants to be called 'cute' and worse than that, have his family jewels considered 'adorable'.* Whether we like it or not, most men measure much of their worth by size: how big a diamond he bought for his girl, how big his staff is and how big his penis is. Like it or not, the amount of confidence men have as businesspeople, as husbands, boyfriends, fathers and friends is often and perhaps unfortunately tied directly to the amount of their vertical and horizontal height. Yes, whether it's your personal preference or not, let's admit it: In our society, size does matter.

## Creativity Kills

Speaking about quantity versus quality, let's look at a different aspect that is more about us girls. A self-created obstacle I see often with my clients and friends is their abundance of creative energy. Yes, I said obstacle because with unbridled creativity comes lack of focus. I've spoken to so many entrepreneurial women's groups and each time, many of the attendees come prepared with their notebooks that they consider their business diaries. They take notes, jot down ideas and make plans through the pages until they have an entire volume of things that never will or can get done. While the ideas are all probably good ones, what the collection really does is create guilt and denial. One woman said to me that the reason she is not successful is that she just keeps having new great ideas. New? Yes. Great? No. Those additional ideas only stall and distract her from accomplishing any one of them.

Focus is paramount to getting all the brain cells working together, to call the laws of attraction (if you believe in them) together for support and, most importantly, to demonstrate your own commitment to yourself and others. With that commitment you can get help from others and inner strength to push through obstacles rather than jumping to the next page of your idea journal. There has to be real will for there to be a way. Focus is the key. While creativity is fun and welcome in the right context, it can also be a business killer for many women who take on too much and complete too little.

For example, I recently met a woman at one of my presentations who asked me if she somehow could create a business around her talents which included graphic design, astrology, bookkeeping and writing. I guess she can write a bookkeeping tool that includes astrological pictures, but I am not sure it would sell. (Can I tell the IRS I can't pay taxes this month because Venus isn't aligned with Mars?) So no, my advice to her and women like this: Pick the thing you enjoy but that you also believe can make money so you can fill your savings account first. This then allows you to have hobbies which make your life full and fascinating. As long as they remain hobbies and not work, your hobbies will remain fun, too.

I've done this myself. I used to be a marketing consultant while I tried to bootstrap a child safety business. I wrote articles for magazines, published my first book and spoke at various conferences about marketing and child safety (not at the same time though!). Not only was I exhausted and poor, I literally led two different lives. My friends and colleagues couldn't really help me as they didn't know who I was anymore or what I was working on. I was a moving target of personalities all the time and, as such, it was hard for potential clients to hire me. I wasn't the best in any one thing even if I was very good in several. I kept hearing the words of a former boss, "Utility players are great to have on a team but they are the first to get cut because when we need a first baseman, we want the best." That statement was hurtful to me as a 24-year-old whippersnapper, but it lingers 20+ years later to remind me that *trying to be something to many really means being nothing to no one.* Perhaps we are afraid of not belonging to any one thing so we try to cover our "bases" by trying to belong to a number of teams.

*"The worst enemy to creativity is self-doubt."*

— Sylvia Plath

Maslow would say that until we fulfill our need to belong, we can't be creative. To deal with this, we join business groups online and in person. We look to others in similar situations for support and advice. We rely on our families to deal with our ups and downs as we create and destroy our own ideas and actions. We sabotage our own success and failure by moving on to the next great thing. And we thrive on other people asking, "So what are you up to *these* days?" It is how we choose to belong in the business world which is tough, unforgiving and alienating. It seems easier to stay on the surface than swim with the sharks. But perhaps it's just easier to keep moving than commit and fail to belong.

**Your Friends Are Not Your Customers**

I hope you have people in your life that you trust and that respect you. Perhaps at some point, you've run a business idea by a friend or family member. 34.6% of women in our survey have done that, too. Whether it was a new revolutionary invention or a way to improve the world, more than likely, your friend/relative had one of two reactions. She told you it was great or that it stunk.

If she told you it was a great idea, she was seemingly positive. Whether she really thought so or not, she told you she liked your idea because she did not want to risk hurting your friendship by telling you what she may really have felt. So while you were seeking feedback, what you were really seeking was support and she delivered it.

The opposite possible reaction is that your friend/relative pooped on your idea. She told you it was a bad idea and questions why you would do that. You may have tried to assuage her with more explanation or tried to help her see it from your perspective. You may have left the discussion depressed and defeated or even disappointed by her lack of support. Just remember our statistic from earlier that almost 91% of the women said they've also had their great ideas and accomplishment bubbles burst by loved ones. And by the way, 61% of people polled by *Parade* magazine said they would choose a different career if they could do it all again. Indeed resentment and jealousy could be behind other people's reaction to your cool new idea.

Maybe more important to note here is that everyone has a different perspective. You would think as a professional marketer, I would be very much in favor of getting market data and asking for people's opinions before you pursue an idea and spend time and money. In general, I am but you have to be careful not to be swayed by small survey samples, especially when they include friends and family.

You know that opinions are cheap and easy — everyone has one and most people love to give them away. Remember my friend who questioned who would buy this book? When I asked her if she ever read *The Secret*, she had no idea what I was talking about. Luckily, several millions of people did. Thousands more watched the movie version, too. Was my friend concerned about me wasting my time writing a book no one would want to buy? I do believe that is true. However, her limited knowledge about what other people want and buy made her feedback less relevant to me (though I admit that at first, I got very defensive!).

A second thing to realize when asking friends and family for feedback is the "it's only you" factor. Since they know you, how could you possibly do something enormously important, ultimately earth shattering, and otherwise famously respected? Think about someone you know who holds an important position at a company or has other impressive credentials. If you know them well, you can't possibly think about them objectively. They'll always be mom, dad, Alyssa or whoever you knew before they had any importance. Therefore, you don't appreciate what other people see and appreciate in that person. Ergo, you really can't give them market-worthy feedback. You are too close to them to represent the market's perspective.

So be sure you know where the feedback is coming from. Discount the negativity and listen for the good questions and points. Pity the person who lacks the confidence to be helpful by providing honest, interested feedback. And, most importantly, don't be discouraged if you really do think your idea has merit. One person's opinion isn't necessarily right. Seek out others, preferably not so biased ones.

I know so many entrepreneurs that validated their concept and even got seed money from friends and family. When the venture failed to produce real customers, they came up with excuses such as, being ahead of the curve, competition, etc. Few admitted that friends and family were saving face by being nice. In order to get real market validation, you need to ask the market — that is, people who could and would pay for your products or services. That is scary. What if the market doesn't like what you have to offer? Isn't it better to know sooner? Of our survey friends who started a business after getting their friends' or relatives' support, 25% of them overall failed and close to 38% of the older entrepreneurs' ventures failed. Don't let your family and friends coddle you into believing they are your customers.

## Alibis and Apologies

Here is something you can do immediately that will improve your professional (and personal) well-being. Stop apologizing.

Consider this: when a woman has to change an appointment or set one up, she will often explain why in great detail. "I have to take my son to football and then drive my daughter to art. Then with traffic I probably can't meet you until 6." "I am sorry, but I have to reschedule our meeting, Paul. I am having some bad abdominal pain so I have to go to my doctor." TMI (too much information)! In contrast, a guy will simply say, "Can't make the meeting. We'll have to reschedule."

If you're in business, when someone asks you how much you charge for your product or service, do you tell them squarely or offer a price that is clearly negotiable? I am often saddened when a woman answers my pricing question and then immediately tells me she is willing to lower it before I even respond to the initial offer. She is probably thinking that she should get me as a customer with the low price and then she can increase the price later. Or perhaps she is really desperate for the business and can't afford to lose the sale. Maybe she didn't do her competitive homework and doesn't know if she offers something of market value. These are legitimate reasons, but I bet most of the time, the reaction and response is really indicative of a women's lack of confidence that her product or service, is, in fact, worth the stated fee. L'Oréal spokeswomen flaunt, "Because I'm worth it"...well excuse me! Who said that the rest of us aren't?

Why do women feel so obligated to give alibis and apologies? It's because we don't want to compromise our belonging. That is, when we must reschedule a meeting, we realize that the other person agreed to meet us; thus, they viewed us as important enough to make time and, therefore, we belonged. When we have to change that, we want to be clear it's not that we don't want to meet but that we can't just then and don't want that person to think otherwise. We want another chance! You then have to almost sell yourself again to get that meeting rebooked — and that is exhausting. Plus, it's also a bad business strategy. By exposing all that information, you give away more information to that person than he or she may be interested in or should know. By being strong and simply stating you can't make the meeting, you make it clear that for you, something else is more important than that meeting. Ironically, this often makes that person question her own belonging to your priorities and can trigger her to be even more eager to reschedule with you. Of course, it depends on who this is. However, if and when you need to reschedule something, consider holding back details. It's hard to do for many women, but yet quite empowering.

## Cool is Sexier than Passionate

While not every woman is outwardly passionate, successful business women tend to be high energy and they work with intensity. They are opinionated and aggressive, which sometimes labels them high maintenance or, stereotypically, bitchy. So here's the truth. That is not good.

Any negotiating class or management training will tell you that it's a better tactic to hold your cards tighter instead of flaunting them all over. Pouring out your guts to people and complaining about things doesn't win you friends or fans. It makes you whiny. We know that, but we sometimes forget it in business.

Entrepreneurs especially need to be careful because they are often told to be passionate about their companies lest no one else will. However, passion often gets translated to mean arrogance, obstinacy or ignorance. Passionate people can be hard to communicate with because they don't keep an open mind about new ideas or criticisms. Passion can be scary or just plain annoying to some and thus can turn off potential investors, customers or employees. Cool confidence is a much better sales tool.

In all things business, consider what you do by Maslow's measure. It will help you see the value of what you have to sell as well as how you must act as an employer and supplier. With all things motivated by belonging, assume the position of awesomeness. No one has the right or data to prove you otherwise, and they'll simply want to jump on your bandwagon so they don't miss the chance to belong to something utterly important...you!

## Girl Talk Guidelines

1. Are you uncomfortable selling your products or services? Do you have to justify the price when asked 'how much'? Why?

2. Do you feel compelled to explain why you need to reschedule appointments? Why?

3. Has anyone ever approached you with a business idea that you thought was bad? Did you tell him/her the truth? How did he/she react?

4. How and why did you select your career path? How would you do it differently if you could? What advice would you give a young person pondering his/her future career?

# Ms. chief

## Promote yourself

We all need to feel loved and that we belong. It's good to know that you aren't alone in the way you feel and act — especially when you do a bonehead thing or it's done to you. I see the same insecurities in virtually every woman, regardless of age, race, experience and education.

The survey data confirms that we live in an age that is information rich and subsequently confidence poor. You would be very hard pressed to find another woman who has the inner confidence to love herself and those around her without expectation. We see and hear so much about other people that we perpetually think we are insignificant and unlucky. The world is always better elsewhere as we fail to see that everyone's lives are challenged. Some people just cope and hide it better.

### Smile and Say Cheese...We Also Do Improve with Age

As women, it seems our toughest years are 40-60 when we start questioning our purpose and accomplishments in sync with our partners, friends and other relations. As such, our own mid-life crisis is as real and potentially damaging as men's where we want to make sweeping change and live as fully as we can, while we can. Thus, we saw big differences in our 40-60 year old survey responses in terms of their confidence, satisfaction and happiness.

The comforting fact is that we do tend to get happier and more confident as we age. A Gallup poll confirmed what our study found as well. Women that are over 50 in the Gallup study, as well as women over 60 in our study, were by and large happier than younger women. They attributed their satisfaction to all kinds of things including solid families, marriages, religious faith and good jobs. These women wouldn't trade in their husbands and they didn't consider having affairs. It's impossible to know if these claims were true or not. Maybe they are happy now because they were still sexually active, maybe because they already sowed their rebellious seeds, or perhaps they have conceded on being happy with what they have and who they are.

William James noted, "True wisdom is the art of knowing what to overlook." Alyssa Dver (me) adds that true wisdom is something you can only learn with time and experience. Now that you know more about Maslow and the importance of that belonging layer, you can perhaps overlook more things as standard human insecure behavior and just move on. Let it roll off your back next time you or someone you know does something really selfish.

Know in your head and in your heart that you are talented, loving, hard-working, careful and well-intentioned. Now you know that sh*t happens to everyone, and happens often. You aren't being singled out and often it's not even due to something you did or didn't do. It's just due to other people's desire to belong.

I don't want to tell you what to do or who to be, but my mission with this book is to help you cope and eliminate some stress from your life. Therefore, it wouldn't be complete without some hopefully wise ideas, if not advice:

### 1. Make someone's day every day.

Go out of your way to say something nice to someone every day.

Do it for whatever reason you need — whether it's to get them to do something for you or just to exercise kindness. Be deliberate and sincere.

Compliment his/her hair or clothes, tell she/he that the person did something really great or even that he/she made *your* day. Give a gift of momentary happiness to someone else and see how it not only pays you forward, but it will actually make you feel good about yourself.

Too easy or obvious? Try it and see how it feels.

Do it to one of your kids, your neighbor, your friend or a total stranger. If you're feeling really brave, try it on someone who isn't usually nice to you and see how that may change. A simple smile sometimes works but it's even better to say something unexpected to him/her that makes that person literally stop and decide how to best respond.

**2. Be interested to be interesting.**

Always try to go second in a conversation.

When asked "How are you?" say, "I'm great but, more importantly, how are you?" Then really listen to that person's answer and ask more questions. "How are your kids?" "Did you take any good trips lately?" "How's your job going?", etc. If you don't know that person and want to build rapport quickly, ask about something they are wearing or doing: "I like that scarf you are wearing. I'd love to get one for my mother-in-law", "Whatever you are working on sure looks challenging.", "My daughter is considering a career in law enforcement, and I am interested to know if you enjoy it."

OK, call this schmoozing and maybe even superficial but if you really listen, you may be surprised at how interesting that person is after all. Your interest initially may only be to get that person to open up and give you data that is really helpful to get inside her head, but I think that is fair motivation. What you want to do is to convey quickly to that person you are interested in *her/him*. That will build respect and a sense of trust from that person to you. That helps grease the skids for anything you need or want later on. Equally important, that builds an "interest IOU" so that the other person will be more intent on listening to you because it's now his/her turn.

Again, this may seem too easy and obvious. Try it. Listening is possibly the best asset in negotiation, relationships, leadership and parenting. We usually don't do it well, and then we can't understand why no one listens to us.

### 3. Be the friend, mother and relative you wish you had.

Once, my son did a bad thing in school that the teacher called home about. I questioned my son by asking, "Do you think that is something Dad or I would do?" He said no and learned to think about appropriate social behavior by emulating someone he wants to be like. Unfortunately, applying this filter to everyday life isn't that easy. At least in hindsight, it can help.

As such, consider the friends, mother and relatives you wish you could have. What would they be like and what would they do for you? While they might not necessarily appreciate the same things in return, you'll know you did the right thing by using your own experience to make better decisions.

For example, if you remember being yelled often by your mother, remind yourself about that next time you do it to your kids. If you got mad last time someone didn't include you for a girls' night out, don't plan the next one and omit that person in revenge. Include her and stand taller by doing what you wished she had done for you. If a friend or relative reacted negatively to one of your brilliant ideas, be cordial and supportive despite it.

Living well is indeed the best revenge. Even if the other person never knew she let you down, you know you are a better person for not belaboring the issues and lowering yourself to that standard (or lack thereof).

Lead by example and live by your own definition of what you want others to be like to you. And when they don't, feel sorry for them as it is their insecurities coming out, not yours.

### 4. Don't take yourself too seriously.

We all do boneheaded things. We all have gaps in our confidence. We all lose perspective of what is really important. Just remember, we all put our pantyhose on the same way, one leg at a time — and once in a while they get ugly, annoying and costly runs even despite our careful efforts.

Everyone is attracted to people who are funny or at least fun. As humans, we want to be part of that party train. Obviously someone who is enjoying herself must be on the right track. People tell me money attracts money. I don't doubt this but even without money, confidence attracts everyone. When it's real and understated, it is by far the most powerful way to win friends and influence others.

Therefore, laugh at yourself or at least stop beating yourself up for things that are just plain uncontrollable. You will make mistakes like saying something thoughtless. Plus, you will consider all the good things you could have done and didn't. What you can control is your attitude. Be positive and be sure. You are as good as the next woman and perhaps better if you act deliberately and reflectively.

Aim for no regrets and practice the art of apologizing when you screw up, not when you need to control your life and priorities. You don't necessarily have to act your age but take advantage of the experiences you have acquired and share the wisdom through your actions so others can learn too.

Most importantly, enjoy the ride. Hopefully it will now have fewer stress-inducing speed bumps that make you wonder why no one prepared you to wear a better bra for your brain. Life is challenging in so many ways that we continue to get emotional concussions from things that our male counterparts seem to avoid. Clearly, we put even more stress on ourselves as women because we care and need to be cared for. This is the good and bad news since it makes us the vulnerable, bitchy, loving, moody women we are. Just remember the Maslovian cause when we do wicked things to ourselves or to other people, or when they are done to us. Now you understand why and you know that it's because everyone is totally full of "bull-longing."

Conclusively, congratulations!

*You were never broken and you are no longer misinformed.*

*You are now part of the Ms. Informed community where every wise woman unconditionally and forever belongs.*

## Girl Talk Guidelines

1. List three things you are really good at.

2. Is there someone in your life that you go to or could go to when you have those bad days that would remind you how wonderful you really are?

3. Who inspires you? Who do you envy? Why?

4. When was the last time you consciously tried to make someone happy? When was the last time someone did that for you?

# Ms. acknowledged

## Public thanks to the greatest people in my world

May you find people in your life that really do make you feel blessed. I include this page here solely to thank my own personal heroes for their contributions to this book and to my life, in general.

To Laurie Cote who designed the cover, page layout and all things Ms. Informed. She is a person extraordinaire both as a business person, women and friend. Her incredible spirit and attitude are only matched by her talent and professionalism. Laurie, you are a true diamond and being around you makes us all glisten.

To Ian DeRanieri, my business manager, who continues to be patient and yet critical despite my technical fits and Maslovian doubts. His unbridled confidence and determination continue to energize and comfort me as this adventure unfolds.

To my husband and children who are beyond supportive and snuggli-cious. I am the luckiest mom and wife and just wish I could perpetually convey my love to them without tattooing it on their bodies.

To Marco Emrich who always will be my mentor, my advocate and number one 911.

To Peter Fingar who taught me about publishing and how to be a business mensch.

To my sister, Jen, for her better sense of humor and level headedness.

And, to my lifeline friends: Jo-Ann Ross, Angela Stinnett and Mary Lou Rogan. Your ongoing morale support, mutual love of wine and food, on-demand humor and unconditional friendship keeps me belonging.

Greg Geracie, you were so selflessly helpful. Thanks to you and to Therese for the connection.

So may others have encouraged and enabled me to do this: Devin C., Diane D., Melody B., Bob V., my mom and aunt La.

And last, but most certainly critical to this book and me, are my reviewers who I put in a terrible predicament asking for their time and honesty! Special shout outs to: John and Julie Rafferty for their very valuable editing and input. Nicole Connolly who provided great feedback as well as the photos on the back cover; Alyce O'Connell for my impromptu head shot; Karen DeMeo Faulkner, who has lovingly told me like it is since kindergarten; Lisa Phipps who not only keeps my Friday night gym workouts bearable, but was a truly helpful editor; and to Ginger Burr who was so gracious and graceful in her review and unique perspective. And to Alicia L., Rachel D., Lori S., Gail W., Heather J., — love you gals! I am Ms. Placed without you!

## About the Author

*Alyssa Dver*

Alyssa's audience members leave laughing, crying and kvetching with one another. But, more importantly, they are all instantly able to live with less guilt, less stress and more energy.
Amen sisters!

A seasoned author and speaker, Dver has polished her performances before producing her Ms. Informed masterpiece. She ignites women's and business groups including the Diversity Summit at the UN, Downtown Women's Clubs, Ladies Who Launch, SuperMompreneur, and oodles more. She is frequently Ms. Quoted as an expert in print, radio, TV, WebTV and online media. Even her own articles often get Ms. Construed by the editors of BusinessWeek, Forbes, Entrepreneur, Chief Marketer and many others that have published her work. American Express and BusinessWeek have recognized her entrepreneurial accomplishments despite her Boardroom Wharton training. Her businesses success includes the recession-defying consulting firm Mint Green Marketing and her do-it-yourself book, No Time Marketing.

When she is not evangelizing about woman's confidence, Alyssa delights in her two delicious sons and eccentric rescue pooch. A competitive badminton player and BodyCombat addict, she uses these to offset her enthusiasm for wine, beer and most any food. She lives in the Boston area with her unusually patient husband, despite being native New Yorkers with bad attitudes about pizza, bagels and the letter "R".

Breinigsville, PA USA
06 April 2011
259333BV00001B/3/P

9 780983 392705